Brown Honey in Broomwheat Tea

Poems by Joyce Carol Thomas

illustrated by Floyd Cooper

HarperCollins*Publishers*

Brown Honey in Broomwheat Tea
Text copyright © 1993 by Joyce Carol Thomas
Illustrations copyright © 1993 by Floyd Cooper
Printed in the U.S.A. All rights reserved.
Typography by Elynn Cohen
1   2   3   4   5   6   7   8   9   10
❖
First Edition

Library of Congress Cataloging-in-Publication Data
Thomas, Joyce Carol.
    Brown honey in broomwheat tea : poems / by Joyce Carol Thomas ;
illustrated by Floyd Cooper.
         p.   cm.
    Summary: A collection of poems exploring the theme of African-
American identity.
    ISBN 0-06-021087-7. — ISBN 0-06-021088-5 (lib. bdg.)
    1. Afro-Americans—Juvenile poetry.   2. Children's poetry, Ameri-
can.   [1. Afro-Americans—Poetry.   2. American poetry.]
I. Cooper, Floyd, ill.   II. Title.
PS3570.H565B7   1993   91-46043
811' .54—dc20   CIP
                                                                    AC

for Aurora Pecot with love
—JCT

for Velma
—FC

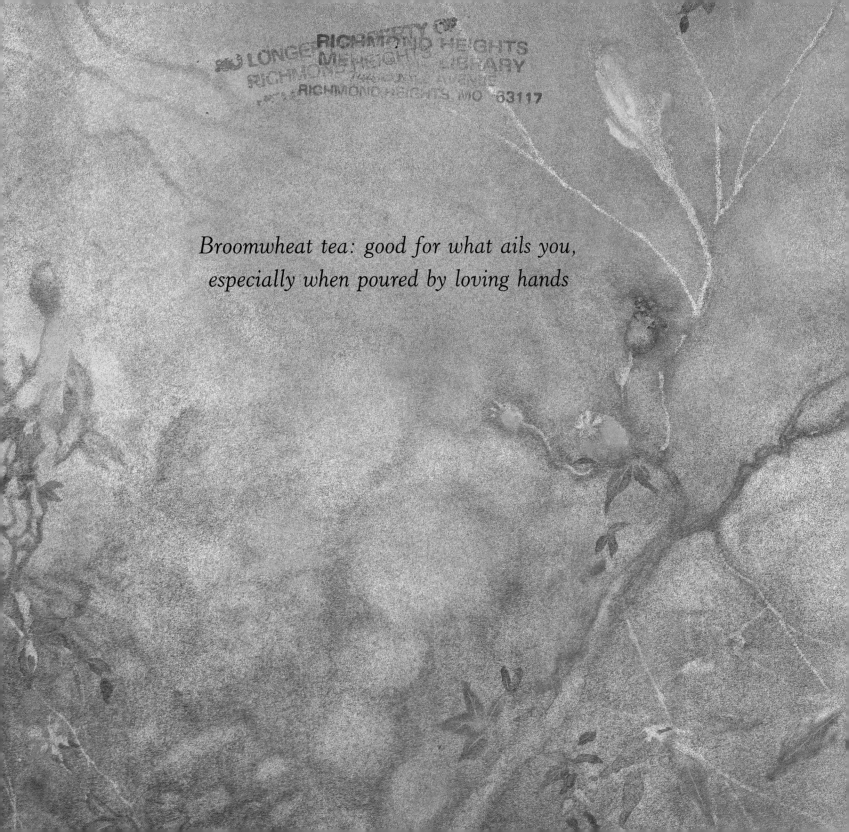

Broomwheat tea: good for what ails you,
especially when poured by loving hands

Cherish Me

I sprang up from mother earth
    She clothed me in her own colors
I was nourished by father sun
    He glazed the pottery of my skin
I am beautiful by design
    The pattern of night in my hair
    The pattern of music in my rhythm
As you would cherish a thing of beauty
    Cherish me

Brown Honey in Broomwheat Tea

My mother says I am
Brown honey in broomwheat tea
My father calls me the sweetwater
      of his days
Yet they warn
There are those who
Have brewed a
Bitter potion for
Children kissed long by the sun
Therefore I approach
The cup slowly
But first I ask
Who has set this table

Magic Landscape

Shall I draw a magic landscape?
In the genius of my fingers
I hold the seeds.
Can I grow a painting like a flower?
Can I sculpture a future without weeds?

Tea Pot

I am the pot that brews the potion

I take my time about boiling

Cozying up to the fire just so

I taste the water when I glow

Then inhale the stems, the twigs

    and every crushed flower

Fragrant in their golden power

I feel so good

Finally

I sing

Mama

I see her walking in the broomweed
Out in the pasture, windy with birds
She's checking the blooms on the weaving heads
The prairie stalks buoyant as her body
Moving up and down the red clay fields
Look there, golden ones ready for reaping
She bows to the plant for permission
Prunes a small twig
Carries it like a healing flower
Over and over the rising road
Branching
Like the divining lines
     in her
      harvest hands

Family Tree

I step into this green forest
Purple with growing roots
This forest down by the blue-green water
That first separated us
       Mother from son
       Father from daughter
       Sister from sister
I look closely at this leaf
I see the branches of these
Woods stepped on, broken
My brothers, and me
       I look across water
And cry for our trembling
       Family tree

Hide Me in the Cradle of Your Love

Oh hide me in the crevice of a rock

Some safe place

Hide me in the cradle

Of your love

In the nook of your warmest

      glance

On some healing shore of

The sea of

      time

I Am a Root

I am hewn from

  the solid ledge of rock

  the soaring songs of birds

  the rocking motions of the ocean

  the uplifted branches of the tree

I am a root

  that will be free

Sisters

The gold dust twins
They call us
Because we are so dark
And all the time I'm thinking
It's the dust from the yellow flowers
sequining the Moroline, Vaseline
on our shiny legs
as we run red, ashless
through the golden weeds

Bitter

Sometimes the broomwheat is bitter
And the cupboards are bare
No money, little food
And the honey in the pot is hiding
My mother and father's eyes
   stay on the sky
      as though
Waiting for the bees to hum
   What if the bees don't come?
      Is a question, is a tornado
      stopped up in my throat

*H*oney

The fields are emerald now
  Royal with birds
  the bees hum loud enough
    to remind us
They've always known
Ice melts
Gray skies turn blue and
Honey's been here long
  before we opened our mouths to drink
And will be forever and ever

Becoming the Tea

Brown honey and broomwheat tea
Sweetwater, Daddy calls me
Liquid ambrosia with fire
"Be careful what you
       ponder," Granny smiles,
"Over a cup of steaming leaves
       for it will surely come to pass."
So I think on
       joy, love, peace,
       patience, grace
Yet I'm sometimes
       impatient, sad, angry,
       awkward
But like the steeping brew
The longer I stand
The stronger I stay

A spoonful of thought and time
helps keep a brood growing
A cup of loving kindness
helps keep a family going